THE MORTGAGE MATRIX

"Lies, Cheats & Deceptions…
The Ugly Truth About Your Bank"

Kelly R. Rivas

KELLY R. RIVAS

The Mortgage Matrix

Copyright © 2012 *A Little Publishing Company*
Cover Design by: Laura Shinn
Formatted by: Laura Shinn
ISBN–13: 978-0-615-68923-4
LCCN: 2012915713

A Little Publishing Company books may be ordered through book-sellers or by contacting:

A Little Publishing Company
Hollywood, CA
www.alittlepublishingcompany.com
1-240-350-9234

Because of the nature of the Internet, any web addresses or links contained in this book may have changed since publication and may no longer be valid.

The views expressed in this work are solely those of the author and do not necessarily reflect the views of the publisher, the publisher hereby disclaims any responsibility for them.

www.ingramcontent.com/pod-product-compliance
Lightning Source LLC
Chambersburg PA
CBHW070810210326
41520CB00011B/1902

ACKNOWLEDGEMENTS

I'd like to thank the many supporters who gave me the encouragement and motivation to keep on doing what I do best.....awakening that fighting spirit! My husband would agree with you most...lol, but I'd like to thank my wonderful half for putting up with me and my dramatics in my bouts with the banks! He's my backbone, my strength and the reason why I am strong today!

I'd like to thank my kids Jordan, Scarlett and Baby E for being patient and realizing their mother is a workaholic, but always had time for our reoccurring strolls through the mall...

A special thank you to my parents for providing me with the genes of a bull.....I am relentless when it comes to fighting for what I believe in. You have shown me that I can achieve anything with hard work, strong work-ethic persistence and dedication. It has lead me down paths that I NEVER thought I could obtain.

To my supportive sisters Tammie, Kim, Linda and sister- in- law Linda. Aka "Voices of Reason" without these strong and influential woman in my life where would I be????? I love you gals more than you know and appreciate you always standing behind me in good times and when life is just rough all over!

A warm thank you to my clients for making my position as fun and exciting as it has been. You have given me a reason to continue my fight against the banks and their unaggressive approach to approving loan modifications! A gracious thank you to LaShaun O'bryant who has not only been a loyal client, but a mentor, a friend and one who has always been there to listen to my ideas, goals and dreams. To Jaime Contreras who has invested in my knowledge and truly believed in me for over 12 years and counting! A client, a friend and a business partner thanks again for putting your faith in me to get the job done!

This book represents our future as we are all in this together. Let's continue to focus on our dreams and never give up the fight.....I SURE WON'T!

TESTIMONIALS

I have never been more stressed out in my entire life more than I have been trying to complete a loan modification. I paid an attorney's office to assist me after my husband had lost his job and not only did I rarely hear from the office, they came back with a denial stating I made too much money! I was livid! I called my bank and they told me I could do the mod myself and asked me to send in my paperwork. I did just that was DENIED once again! I was speaking to one of my clients and she told me she worked with Kelly and that she was able to get hers through. I called Kelly the next day and not only was she able to get my modification through...during the process she gave me status several times a month and was very professional. I can't thank her enough for taking this stress away from us! We have recommended her to many people and would recommend her to many more! Thanks so much Kelly!
- Alva C.

I am a real estate investor with many properties. Kelly was able to obtain approvals on all of my investment homes. The process was great and it didn't take that long. She sent me status reports via email and I am forever grateful. My tenants weren't making the entire monthly mortgage payment and I always came out of my pocket each month, but now that the homes are modified I am actually making money each month. My overall experience with this company has been a pleasant one and I would recommend her, and have recommended her to many people. I am a very satisfied client and can't thank her enough for making this process this easy.
- LaShaun O.

I am a business owner, and in a perfect world, this would be great. However, after the economy took a nose dive so did my business. The once booming store I owned became quiet and unprofitable. I lost a lot of money and was barely able to pay my bills. In addition, my husband lost his job after working for 30 years. He was laid off and in the midst of a hip replacement, we couldn't afford to pay our mortgage, and were late many months prior to finding Kelly. A client highly recommended her to me as he knew we were struggling. Little did I know meeting her would change our lives. She was able to modify my payment from 2400.00 down to 700.00 for a permanent mod at 2% for 30 years. This approval came to me as a shock as I had already paid another company to modify and they took the money and I NEVER received an approval. We are thrilled and even though we took a hit financially, we are able to afford our payment. Thank you, thank you, thank you.....
- Vancella B.

I was approved for a modification and wanted to write in to thank you. Your hard work, dedication to my file and your professionalism showed throughout my process. I highly recommend people use this service if they want a low payment. I was able to go from 2800.00 down to 900.00. This program is incredible and should be used all over the nation. If anyone needs a verbal recommendation I will gladly sign up.
-Veronica E.

TABLE OF CONTENTS

THE MORTGAGE MATRIX
"Lies, Cheats & Deceptions…
The Ugly Truth About Your Bank"

Kelly R. Rivas

Published by
A Little Publishing Company
Hollywood, California

HELP... WHAT IS A LOAN MODIFICATION?

Today, about 7.5 million U.S. households are behind on their mortgage payments, and one in four borrowers are underwater on their mortgage, owing more on their mortgage than what their home is worth.

Millions of American homeowners can no longer afford their mortgage payments. As a result, the Obama administration has set up a housing relief program, which aims to put borrowers into more affordable loans to help them avoid foreclosure (HAMP) But the programs have gotten off to a slow start. Many borrowers continue to face obstacles when trying to obtain a loan modification because banks are overwhelmed and understaffed. The Loss Mitigation and Home Retention departments are under-informed about new government and in-house programs designed to help borrowers. Therefore, we have found that the majority of Customer Service Reps are wage earners are only there for a paycheck. The people on the other end of the phone can provide no more information than the man on the moon. Their title appears to be a "go between" or a middle-man between our clients and the underwriter. Their roll is minimal and rather than trying to assist clients in obtaining a loan modification we find they are better at losing paperwork, providing fax numbers that are changed abruptly, reading from a computer screen, or under informed about

what is going on with the file prior to conversing with us....
and then the laziness kicks in. Instead of providing a warm
transfer sadly enough our borrowers end up getting lost in
phone-tree hell.

The Obama administration's, Making Home Affordable
program, was looking like another government failure, but like
any new program, there is a learning curve for both the lenders
and the borrowers. It's numbers have improved sharply, with
650,000 borrowers obtaining trial loan modifications and
375,000 eligible to convert to permanent modifications by the
end of the year, and today the administration is stepping up
pressure on banks to complete even more loan modifications.
With the new Department of Justice program coming on the
scene we have been able to assist clients with obtaining loan
modifications more quickly. The down side to this program is
that it will only benefit some clients and will only benefit
clients who hold mortgages with the top 5 banks that were
named in the lawsuit. JP Morgan Chase, Bank of America,
Wells Fargo, Ally Financial – formerly GMAC – and Citibank.
The Treasury Department has announced plans to send
"SWAT teams" into the largest mortgaging servicing
companies to work hand in hand with mortgage executives to
boost their success rates.

The term "loan modification" is becoming increasingly familiar
to homeowners as adjustable rates come due, property values
fall, and economic uncertainty persists. As housing sales have
fallen and mortgage re-financings have almost become void,
loan modifications are the only indicator standing between
millions of homeowners and the prospect of losing their homes
to foreclosure.

Simply put, a loan modification is a negotiated transaction between a borrower and the current lender on that borrower's mortgage. A home loan modification is a negotiated change made to an existing home loan by a home loan modification specialist that effectively reduces the home loan payments to an amount that the home owner can better afford to pay. The payment is reduced to 31 percent of the home owner's gross income, and so the program is therefore only really of any use to those home owners who have home loan payments that exceed 31 percent of their monthly gross income. The specific purpose of a loan modification is to bring the borrower's monthly mortgage payments back in line with his or her current financial situation.

What is the point of a home loan modification?

If protecting your credit score is a factor in your decision to make a home loan modification, then homeowners who are delinquent on their home loan payments should note that they have already experienced an impact on their credit score. However, this impact is significantly lower than the impact that a foreclosure will have. Working with a home loan modification specialist can help homeowners to maintain their property, and to prevent their credit score from taking any additional hits.

The specific effect of a loan modification on your credit score depends on how the bank reports the modification to the credit bureau. It is possible and advisable to request that the bank report the change to the loan as a loan adjustment, showing on your credit report as a new loan with a lower payment and no increase in the debt structure. Reporting that the modified payment agreement is current will also help to protect your credit rating during the 'trial modification' phase of the home loan modification. Will the trial offer payments show as being late on your credit report? YES. The trial payments are partial payments and will affect your credit. Will the late payments reduce your credit score significantly? Possibly. Generally, when you are late with any payments your score can drop from 50-100 points, however, I have seen both sides of the coin. I have seen where my client with 550 scores remain at about 550 or maybe a 20 point reduction, but nothing outlandish. I will speak more about credit later in this book, but I will say our credit repair team has the ability to fix the issues you may have regarding credit late payments and decreasing scores.

What are the requirements?

The primary requirement for a loan modification is a verifiable financial hardship for the borrowers and 31% of monthly gross income. The hardship must directly relate to the borrower's ability to make payments toward the mortgage on the home in which he or she lives. The HAMP program, which is President Obama's Making Homes Affordable states that you MUST reside in your home in order to qualify for this program. However, many banks have implemented their "own" unique in- house programs to provide everyone a chance to keep their homes, which includes real estate investors.

Hardships include unemployment, loss of income, death, illness, excessive financial responsibilities, and reduction in income.. Once hardship is determined the work can begin to reduce the monthly payments for the borrower.

Many borrowers will initially try to negotiate directly with their lender in a do-it-yourself manner. This is usually an extremely frustrating and unproductive endeavor due to the borrower's lack of knowledge of the loan modification process. At the same time, lenders are reluctant to provide the time, education, and advice in a situation where the lender would be negotiating against itself. Often forgotten is that a mortgage is, in itself, a legal document drawn by the lender with fine print, difficult language, and obligations the borrower might not even be aware of.

While negotiating for themselves is always available to borrowers, a loan modification specialists experience and knowledge of mortgage documents and the negotiation process can make a huge difference in the eventual outcome of a loan modification.

Establishing your mortgage obligation to a comfortable level is accomplished by adjusting one or more of the terms of the mortgage to allow for a reduction in the borrower's monthly mortgage payment. Most, if not all, loan modifications start with a reduction in the interest rate of the borrower's current mortgage. The interest rate reduction can be fixed down to a 2%, however investors who hold your note have the flexibility to set your rate at whatever they see fit. The term generally is for 30 years however, in the past 5 years clients have been introduced to a "step program" or a 5 year program. The "Step Program" may look similar to this:

Year 1 – 2%
Year 2 – 3%
Year 3 – 3%
Year 4 – 4%
Year 5 – caps at 4.875%

If you are currently in one of these programs I would recommend that you resubmit your loan modification package and try for a fixed term of 2% for 30 years. Another method is to extend the borrowers' mortgage beyond its current maturity. A normal extension will take a mortgage from 30 out to 40 years. The combination of an extension with a reduction in interest can result in much lower monthly payments for borrowers.

Lenders are now willing to renegotiate loans due to the possibility of foreclosure and the multiple properties at large. If a deal is possible the negotiators will make it happen for you!

Benefits of Loan Modification

The most common changes are **lowering the interest rates** (down to as low as 2%), **extending the length or your loan** (modifying a 30 year loan to a 40 year loan for example) and even **reducing the principal balance** (the amount you owe the bank).

Another common benefit is either wiping out late fees (which add up fast) or putting them back on the loan balance. This is great for those homeowners who have missed payments and cannot catch up. But remember, if you don't ask, the banks will not perform these actions on their own. You will need to bring all products and programs to their attention. This is the reason to have a specialist who understands the programs. Banks have a "No Ask, No Tell" policy. If you don't bring it to their attention, you may not obtain the assistance you need.

- **Escrows** – If a client has not made a mortgage payment in over a year the escrow account will continue to build in a negative position. In order for the lender to recoup their fees they will do the following:

- **Homeowners insurance** – when a client's insurance becomes due and the borrower is not paying the mortgage, the bank will cover the cost of the insurance, but you WILL pay a high price for it!

- **Taxes** – in order to recoup the fees the bank will take the balance of the taxes owed and amortize over a course of 1 year.

We however, negotiate to reduce the monthly payment even lower. This can be done by extending the tax arrearage to OVER 1 year. We basically, ask the bank to extend to the MAX term which is typically over the course of 4-5 years depending on the bank. This will reduce the monthly payment drastically. These are the two most common ways to reduce your monthly payments and remain my ace in the hole. Why? Because it's a sure bet. What happens to most Americans who do not pay their mortgage during the loan mod process is the bank will take responsibility for taxes and homeowners insurance payments. Because they hold the note for your home they will never leave your property uninsured. BUT....Before you start thinking, "oh how nice of them" please realize there is a method to their madness! The back taxes you owe, once a mod is approved, will be lumped together, divided by 12 and asked that you pay within one year. For those of you who have not paid a mortgage payment for several months realize that what this amount can be extensive. For the banks to ask that you pay the taxes in one year is outrageous considering you would have made the payment faster if they would have completed the modification review faster! However, if you are savvy enough, you may ask the bank to extend that length of time. This will tremendously reduce the monthly payment. Another method to reduce the monthly payment is to obtain your own homeowners insurance. If you do not pay your homeowners insurance policy during the modification process, and your homeowner's policy expires, the lender will pay if for you. It will be 3 times the amount you were paying your prior company. Therefore, prior to your permanent modification make sure you find your own homeowners insurance policy. This new policy must be faxed to the escrow department. Do not give it to the person you were working with in Loss mitigation or Eminent Default. To obtain these two means of reducing your payment is time consuming. It's also imperative that you reach the appropriate departments at the bank or it will never happen. For this reason we handle these two BIG ticket items for you within our process.

The Unfortunate Truth about Loan Modification

If the truth be told the modification process is a tedious one. Numerous amounts of faxing, refaxing and phone calling will be a must for anyone who is thinking of modifying a loan. Months upon months will go by while late fees accrue, monthly payments build up and worst of all most companies will only allow for a trial offer of 3 or 6 months depending on the bank. After the trial payments, luckily your chances of obtaining a permanent modification stand at about 99%. We recommend you do everything in your power to pay these trial payments on time. Once you are late, you will quickly be removed from the trial offer and if you are considering a loan modification your process will start all over again. Once you have made the trial payments continue to make the trial offer payment until hearing from the bank in regards to your permanent modification. This will show affordability and your intentions of making good on your loan.

NO DOESN'T ALWAYS MEAN NO!

The banks make mistakes. No doubt about it. Occasionally, I have clients who receive letters in the mail stating they have been denied. If you receive a denial letter chances are its inaccurate. The banks records are unorganized and misleading. If you are working with a 3rd party company send the correspondence to them immediately so they can call and address the situation. The banks are overwhelmed with files and their process is not solid. If in fact you do receive a denial letter...well guess what? We use the banks denials letters to our advantage. When I see a denial letter it means absolutely NOTHING to me! Please do not be alarmed by this letter as about 98% of the time they are inaccurate. I take the letter, turn it around, send the appropriate documentation back in to the bank and WAHLA!!!! MAGIC HAPPENS!

"DO AS I SAY NOT AS I DO"

Do you remember when you were a kid and your parents used to tell you, "Do as I say not as I do!" Did you seriously know what the heck they were talking about? I used to stand dumbfounded at the fact that I would have to make the determination to listen to my mother or be slapped! I never took the later of the two options. Therefore, I listened up and did the right thing! I do the same to all my clients. Listen up and learn! Listen to what I'm saying or…..now, I would never slap anyone, but I'd be lying if the thought never crossed my mind! Collectively thinking, I take mental note and ask my clients politely if they wouldn't mind sending me EXACTLY what I need. When I say, "send me EXACTLY what I need"….*I really mean it!* Please do so and nobody gets hurt…If not, chances are we might not obtain an approval and more tedious work will need to be done in order to resolve a situation that could have been earlier avoided.

3 Major Reasons why Millions are Foreclosed Upon

- Initial file submission is not accurate

Initial file submission requires specific documents that the bank will need in order to underwrite your file appropriately. And, not only do they need those forms, but they need these forms to be completed accurately. One incomplete detail makes a huge difference. These specific forms can be found online, (or in a copy of our workbook) however, you will need to know which forms to access. Therefore, it's best to contact a professional who will be able to provide you with a detailed checklist. Forms that are not processed properly can set you back weeks sometimes months from an approval!

- Clients wait too long between phone calls

Let's face it. Everyone is busy working, being a parent, paying bills, being the chef, who has time to make calls to the lender? This process is tedious, but weekly phone calls to the lender for status is an absolute MUST!!!! If you do not call the lender on a weekly basis paperwork falls through the cracks. Unfortunately, nobody knows when the underwriter will review your file. The file MUST be kept up-to-date at EVERY point. The paystubs and bank statements MUST be dated within 30 days. If the underwriter picks up the file and the docs are not dated within 30 days your file will be pushed to the bottom of the underwriters stack! Typically the underwriter is responsible for up to 500 files so the next time they review your file can be another month!

- Clients overextend their finances on financial form

Clients tend to overextend their finances to prove they need assistance. In fact, the more monthly expenses you share with your lender the worse off you will be. Be conservative (but truthful) when addressing your monthly responsibilities. This issue is the MAIN DEAL KILLER! The income to expense ratio can make you or break you. If you do not know how to calculate ratios please seek a professional who can assist you through this process.

Contact the OCC

If you're working with a national bank and you believe they're acting unethically, you can file a complaint online with the Office of the Comptroller of the Currency. The OCC charters, regulates and supervises all national banks, and their complaint form can be found online at:
www.helpwithmybank.gov.

Each situation is different and the final decision of eligibility is at the mortgage holder's discretion.

Disclaimer: Loan Modification Central is not affiliated with any financial institution, lender, or bank. Loan Modification Central is a publisher of educational resource materials only. There are no warranties, guarantees or implied results in relation to the outcome of any loan workout application when using materials purchased from Loan Modification Central.

SHORT SALES WITH SHORT MONEY

What is a "Short Sale"?

A **"short sale"** is a sale of real estate in which the proceeds from selling the property will fall short of the balance of debts secured by liens against the property and the property owner cannot afford to repay the liens' full amounts, whereby the lien holders agree to release their lien on the real estate and accept less than the amount owed on the debt.

Any unpaid balance owed to the creditors is known as a *deficiency*. Short sale agreements do not necessarily release borrowers from their obligations to repay any deficiencies of the loans, unless specifically agreed to between the parties.

A short sale is often used as an alternative to foreclosure because it mitigates additional fees and costs to both the creditor and borrower; however both will often result in a negative credit report against the property owner. If this is the case contact us and we will enroll you in our credit restore program to remove the short sale from your report.

Often creditors require the borrower to prove they have an economic or financial hardship preventing them from being able to pay the deficiency. Creditors holding liens against real estate can include primary mortgages, junior lien holders such as: second mortgages, home equity lines of credit (HELOC) lenders, home owners association HOA (special assessment liens), all of whom will need to approve individual applications for a short sale, should they be asked to take less than what is owed.

Most large creditors have special Loss Mitigation or Short Sale departments that evaluate borrowers' applications for short sale approval. Often creditors use pre-determined criteria for approving the borrowers and the terms of the sale of the properties. Part of this process typically includes the creditor(s) determining the current market value of the real estate by obtaining an independent evaluation of the property from an appraisal, a broker price opinion (BPO), or a broker opinion of value (BOV). One of the most important aspects for the borrower in this process is putting together a proper real estate short sale package. The package should be well organized along with a hardship letter explaining to your bank why a short sale is needed.

Depending on each banks policy and the type of loan, creditors may accept applications from borrowers even if the borrower is not in default with their payments. Due to the overwhelming number of defaulting borrowers, mortgage failures and other causes as part of the financial crisis of 2007 to present, many creditors have become adept at processing such short sale applications; however, it can still take several months for the process from start to finish, often requiring multiple levels of approval. If you plan on a short sale it is recommended you hire a 3rd party advocate to handle your paperwork. They will assist you through the entire process initiating your package, submitting it to the bank, and following up until you go to closing. The best part is that you do not have to pay them out of your pocket! The fee can range anywhere from $1,500.00 to $5,000.00 depending upon the amount of work that will be provided to you. This fee is contractual between you and the consulting firm, but you can negotiate with the consultants to have the bank pay them as a part of the closing costs. Take this assistance and run with it! It makes a difference and will take the stress of this process off your shoulders.

How do "Short Sales" Work?

A home is listed "For Sale," like any other traditional listing. During the short sale process, I am asked by many clients, "what will happen if I do not make a mortgage payment during my short sale?" First, you must be approved for short sale. The package that is sent to the lender must make sense and be orderly. Our firm has the ability to keep you out of foreclosure during the short sale process by asking the appropriate department to push the sale date back. (granted, if there is a sale date) Therefore, I quickly respond by saying that "once our package is in process with the lender you will not lose your home for nonpayment". This generally is the truth, however, if the lender decides to not push an auction or trustee's date back, then there is nothing we can do. Once the package is in, the bank will complete a BPO (Brokers Price Opinion) this will enable the bank to obtain an informed idea of what the values are around the subject property. Once the BPO is complete the bank will be ready to receive all offers. Offers that are reasonable to the bank will be considered. Reasonable generally means 20-30% reduction of the current market value. They will easily throw out any low ball offers that folks tend to put into the bank. Once again, there is a method to their madness as they will not entertain low ball offers if they do not make sense or if they will demean the integrity of the subdivision, PUD (Planned Unit Development) or surrounding area.

The home will be active on the MLS (Multiple Listing Service) and MANY other sites (Realtor.com, Homes Data Base, and 350 other sites) in order to sell your home. Agents around the area will find qualified buyers and place an offer on the home. Once the offer is accepted, sit back and wait for your closing date. Once the date arrives the title/escrow company will transfer the proceeds from the buyer's funds to pay off the principle balance that you owe your current mortgage company. There are three MAJOR benefits for selling your home with a short sale. First, homeowner's association dues, water bill, back taxes, judgment liens attached to the home, etc. will be paid off at the time the short sale closes. Second, President Obama has taken an excellent stance on the deficiency folks were once paying. The deficiency is the difference between what you owed the bank (principle balance) and what you sold the property for (sales price).

Example: Your Principle Balance was $ 500,000.00
         Your sold price was $350,000.00
         Your deficiency is: $150,000.00

Generally, you would have been paying taxes on $150,000 (your deficiency) via a 1099 tax payment from the forever gracious IRS.(Internal Revenue Service) not to be confused with the Federal Government as the IRS (Internal Revenue Service) is a separate entity. They work to collect taxes for the US Government, but they are NOT the Government! However, a HUGE thank you to Mr. President Obama for alleviating us of that debt. Our deficiencies have been waived for now, but do take into consideration this may change in the future. Third, there is a new program called "cash for keys" that provide sellers with an incentive to move. The program is definitely not a means to an end, but it assists sellers with moving costs and in some cases it's enough for a down payment on another home. Initially, the HAFA program (cash for keys) assisted sellers with a maximum payout of $3,000.00 given to them at the closing table. However, in today's market, I see sellers obtaining up to $30,000.00 for moving out of their home. If you call the bank and ask them how they come up with the amount you will be given at the closing table....good luck....like anything else with loan modifications or short sales...nobody really knows the formula except for the short sale Gods and they don't have a phone number!

In sum, many clients want to know if they MUST make their payments during the short sale process. Hopefully, this will set the record straight......I have clients who have not made a mortgage payment in OVER 2 years and the banks WILL short sale. It is up to the borrower's discretion if they chose to pay the mortgage during this process as the late payments will negatively impact their credit, but it can be done and payment is not required in order to complete the short sale. This will happen as long as the appropriate package has been submitted to the bank. The package must be maintained in an "up -to – date" manner in order to obtain final approval. Take note that late fees, penalties, and attorney fees will accrue until the sale is complete.

How Do Short Sales Differ From Foreclosures?

Short sales, differ from a foreclosure, in the following 7 ways.

- FICO scores are **NOT impacted** nearly as detrimental with a short sale. While Short Sales have an effect on the home owner's credit, foreclosures often are worse for credit scores.
- A Foreclosure shows the inability to pay, however, many people who have short sold their home were NEVER late on their payments.
- Short sales allow you to remove yourself from an obligation that is up-side-down and obtain the same house at a much lower price.
- **No junior lien holder lawsuits, No Public Auctions, and No evictions** as occurs with foreclosures.
- No costs during or after - **all fees** - are paid by lender.
- Does not hinder employment opportunities as foreclosures can.
- Credit History – If you plan on obtaining a loan in the future, lenders will review the history. If a short sale shows as opposed to a foreclosure, and if your credit has proven to be relatively stable prior to the short sale, the lender will lean more towards your compensating factors. (stability on job, length of time in career, assets, years at each residence, etc.)

The following 11 tips and strategies can put your mind at ease and keep your home off the auction block:

1. Start now: Not so long ago, loan modification was an option reserved only for homeowners who were in default – that is, when their lender filed a motion to start the foreclosure process, usually after 90 days of late payments. Otherwise known as the NOTICE OF DEFAULT. However, if you are NOT late you will still be able to take advantage of the lower interest rates of 2%-4% by way of

EMINENT DEFAULT. This Department was designed to assist clients who are NOT late on their mortgage, and prevent them from becoming late on their mortgage. Does it work? Yes, we have assisted many clients who wished to lower their monthly mortgage payment who have NEVER been late.

2. HAMP, HARP, HARP 2.0, DEPARTMENT OF JUSTICE, IN-HOUSE PROGRAMS. If you are wondering what programs are available....keep in mind each bank has their own policy when it comes to what they offer. Although President Obama has developed programs that are beneficial to many Americans, not all banks (Investors) must participate. We do a thorough scan of all products and programs daily to keep up with the latest and greatest programs so that we may offer our clients the best plan available.

3. Will you need a professional 3rd party advocate?: One of the first questions you need to answer is whether you want to tackle pursuing a loan modification yourself. Should you hire an attorney or a loan-modification firm? Seek help from a nonprofit housing group? The advice varies. You may want to ask yourself, "Are you savvy enough, and do you have the time, to battle these lenders on your own"? The banks work normal business hours and it is highly likely that you will be on the phone for hours per month. Many say spending up to $4,000 on an attorney who's well-versed in these issues can be money well-spent. But are they well-versed? Taking a peek from outside the black box is funny... If you ask an Attorney what you should do he'll say, "File Bankruptcy". If you ask a real estate agent they'll say, "short sale", if you ask a Loan Broker they will

say, "refinance". So where do you go from there? In my personal opinion if you enjoy your home....then try everything you can to keep it! Here are the honest answers, in order and why....(1) Refinance (2) Loan Modification (3) Short Sale. First you must understand your options and why you will need to select them in this order. (4) Deed in Lieu.

A. Refinance – there are programs available if you are underwater. Unfortunately, the only loans that will qualify, however, are loans that are held by Fanniemae or Freddiemac or government loans. Go to www.fanniemae.com/loanlookup to see if you qualify. Also, try www.freddiemac.com. If your loan is held by a private investor....all I can say is, "sorry your investor has not jumped on the band wagon and therefore you will not have any refinancing options. If you have a FHA loan STREAMLINE IMMEDIATELY! Even if you are underwater the lender will allow you to refinance. The documentation is easy. No documents are required! No paystubs, no bank statements, nothing....not even an appraisal! Call a loan specialist immediately.

B. Loan Modification – This should be your second option. Loan modifications work. Your package must be set up properly and the information within the package must make sense. Depending on your current interest rate, a loan modification can reduce your monthly payment significantly.

C. Short sale – if you cannot afford your monthly payment and loan modification did not work in your favor a short sale is a sure bet to remove the burden and earn extra cash at closing.

D. Deed in Lieu - A Deed in Lieu is available, but it offers no benefit to the homeowner and is not advisable.

4. There are a number of loan-modification scams out there. A consultation is the best way to get a feeling of how the company may perform. Try to work with a company that gives updates, who is honest, and select a company where someone you know has previously obtained a loan modification.

5. Uncover your lender: Knowing who your lender is may help you get a better modification. These days, your loan is either owned by a single bank or it's been sliced up into tiny pieces and turned into a mortgage-backed security and is owned by many people. If the bank owns the loan, you for sure have the possibility of getting more flexible terms, because they don't have to go anywhere else to get pre-approval. You really don't know what you qualify for unless you know who owns your loan. As the homeowner you should go directly to your mortgage servicer and ask who owns your loan. You can find servicer's phone numbers on your mortgage statement or book of payment coupons.

6. Be honest: As part of an application, it's pertinent to gather your financial information and present it to the lender. Give the lender exactly what they need so the process goes

swiftly. And make sure it's accurate. It can be tempting to bend the truth when you are trying to convince a lender to approve a loan modification. Some homeowners are embarrassed by something they did to place their finances in jeopardy; Others try to fudge the numbers to make themselves eligible for a loan modification they cannot otherwise qualify for. There are certain areas within your financial worksheet that are flexible, but check with a specialist prior to submitting your loan modification package as there is a proper way to balance your income and expense ratios. Now isn't the time for deception or trying to tackle this on your own. Before reaching out to your servicer you'll want to gather the following paperwork:

- Information about the monthly gross (before tax) income of your household, including recent pay stubs if you receive them or documentation of income you receive from other sources.
- Profit and Loss statement for business owners
- Your most recent income-tax return.
- Bank Statements (last two)
- Information about your first or any such loan we would see on a credit report, and a monthly mortgage statement.
- Information about any second mortgage or home-equity line of credit on the house.
- Account balances and minimum monthly payments due on all of your credit cards.
- Account balances and monthly payments on all your other debts such as student loans and car loans.

- A letter describing any circumstances that caused your income to be reduced or expenses to be increased (job loss, divorce, illness, etc.) if applicable.

7. Write the ideal hardship letter: As part of your paperwork, you'll have to write a hardship letter that explains how you entered into a hardship situation. This letter is very important and needs to be written well. Be detailed and pinpoint dates of the hardship and be specific. If the servicer can't understand why you originally fell behind from reading your hardship letter, they may wonder whether there's other things going on that you're not telling them. One common mistake would be (for example) if you lost your job in June and you spent most of the letter discussing how it put you behind, when your finances actually show that they started to fall behind in February. Your letter should be precise in explaining the exact train of events: "His hours at work were cut back in the spring, which led to trouble with the mortgage, which led to more stress and so on". That makes more sense. And lastly, keep it simple and concise because it's easier to read a two-paragraph or three-paragraph letter than a five-page letter.

8. Get the right people on the phone: Homeowners who've had their loans modified report that one of the biggest frustrations is just getting the right person on the phone. If you're trying to do it on your own, the first thing to do – it sounds basic – is just make sure you're talking to the right department. You should be speaking to 'loss mitigation if you are late on your mortgage or "eminent default" if you are not late. Immediately ask for these departments as the call centers pick up the phone.

9. Be realistic: If the lender provides an approval for a loan modification and the payment is ANYTHING less than what you were paying...TAKE IT! This will show the bank you are trying. Do not expect for your mortgage to be cut in half just because your friend down the streets payment was cut. Each case differs by the income and interest rate in which you currently hold. The benefit...is that this payment can be temporary for you. Did you know that the bank will allow you to remodify after 1 year? Take the payment and if you still don't like the payment after 1 year try it again! You can resubmit your package and the bank WILL reconsider.

10. Payment: Consult a loan specialist to assist you with processing your documents appropriately. Through the work you've done with a professional, or through your own number crunching, explain to the bank what payment would work for you. You're not being deceptive or bluffing – you're being honest. Because there are so many homes that lenders do not want on their books, it's a game of poker, and the game is getting better and better for homeowners. Foreclosing is extremely expensive (for lenders), and it's only getting more expensive. Try modifying and submitting your package over and over until you have the payment that best suits your household.

11. Keep your cool: Understandably, homeowners often become frustrated and angry when seeking assistance from their lender. Do I blame you? HECK NO! I work with call centers everyday that represent your investor. Are they knowledgeable? Again, HECK NO! 99.9% of the "so called" account managers have never approved a loan in their lives, do not know how to calculate payments, have no idea

how to calculate ratios, nor do they seem to understand how the underwriter arrives at your approval. Their role is to gather your documents and forward them to the negotiator or "so called" underwriter. Is the account manager there to assist you in obtaining a loan modification? AGAIN, HECK NO! These are hourly rate employee's there to obtain a paycheck! Their knowledge is less than desirable and for that the homeowners will become more and more frustrated. You will hear through the grapevine that industry "people" speak negatively about 3rd parties advising the homeowner to cease communication with their lender. Now, I'm just saying, as a homeowner, if you are not knowledgeable about the modification process and the person on the other end of the phone is not knowledgeable about the process isn't that a case of the blind leading the blind? I feel at least one party on the phone should be knowledgeable and it may as well be us! Therefore, I advise my clients to stay away from the stress and stay away from the call centers who claim they are the "BANK".

12. Call in the politicians: "If you're getting the runaround, don't be afraid to 'CC' your senator or congress man/woman. Unfortunately, we run into some files that clearly are not handled properly. In these cases we go the extra mile. Asking for a Supervisor of a call center will do you no good. They are 3rd party entities with absolutely NO power. You must go for the gusto and contact your banks Corporate Office, get their fax number and then "CC" your State Representatives. Contacting the powers that be is necessary and will put your file in the hot seat!

13. Leave a paper trail: Document everything! Every time you speak to your lender/call center ask for their name and ID number. This will allow the Corporate office to track the employee faster in the event its necessary. Make a file for all your correspondence. Document and write down all conversations that took place with the lender. Example: 'April 13th, I spoke to Bank of America, with employee Jennifer Jones, employee number xxx. Why? Because if you have this, and are facing foreclosure, you can bring this to an attorney and use it to build a solid case. It will show you tried to find a solution. And at the very least, it keeps you incredibly organized during the process. Also, use certified mail and/or shipping companies like FedEx, to ensure that documents arrive safely and that you have proof of it. During the loan-modification process, some lenders may say they never received documents. Make sure you fax and obtain a fax transmittal summary. Call the bank the very next day to make ensure they have received it.

14. Follow up: I read tons of blogs every evening from homeowners that have not been approved, are mad and state they are in a state of fax frenzy! The majority of the homeowner's state they fax, and fax, and fax and then fax some more. Well folks, the reason why homeowners fax so often is because the first time they fax, they don't follow up the next day to make sure the lender had received their fax. If you do not make this a habit. You will be in fax hell like the majority of the folks I read about every night. It's wise to perform a little due diligence when working with your lender. Make absolute sure that the banks have your documentation as it will ensure your file is pushed through appropriately.

15. Patience is not just a virtue, but a necessity: "Most importantly, you've got to have stick-to-it-ism. When they say 'no,' they probably mean they don't know. It takes time to work through the system. A normal modification can take 3 to 12 months, so be very patient. If the paperwork is up-to-date and accurate and the follow up calls to the bank are in every week or two the underwriter WILL review your case.

FORECLOSURES

What is a Foreclosure?

A Foreclosure is a specific legal process in which a lender attempts to recover the balance of a loan from a borrower who has stopped making payments to the lender by forcing the sale of the asset used as the collateral for the loan.

Formally, a mortgage lender (mortgagee), or other lien holder, obtains a termination of a mortgage borrower (mortgagor)'s equitable right of redemption, either by court order or by operation of law (after following a specific statutory procedure). Usually a lender obtains a security interest from a borrower who mortgages or pledges your asset to secure the loan. If the borrower defaults and the lender tries to repossess the property, courts of equity can grant the borrower the equitable right of redemption if the borrower repays the debt. While this equitable right exists for some, it is a mute point for others. This varies by state so it is wise to understand your redemption rights. Contact a specialist to find if your state has a right-of-redemption.

Therefore, through the process of foreclosure, the lender seeks to *foreclose* the equitable right of redemption and take both legal and equitable title to the property in fee simple. Other lien holders can also foreclose the owner's right of redemption for other debts, such as for overdue taxes, unpaid contractors' bills or overdue homeowners' association dues or assessments.

The foreclosure process as applied to residential mortgage loans is a bank or other secured creditor selling or repossessing a parcel of real property (immovable property) after the owner has failed to comply with an agreement between the lender and borrower called a "mortgage" or "deed of trust". Commonly, the violation of the mortgage is a default in payment of a promissory note, secured by a lien on the property. When the process is complete, the lender can sell the property and keep the proceeds to pay off its mortgage and any legal costs, and it is typically said that, "the lender has foreclosed its mortgage or lien". If the promissory note was made with a recourse clause then if the sale does not bring enough to pay the existing balance of principal and fees the mortgagee can file a claim for a deficiency judgment.

What Types of Foreclosures are there?

The mortgage holder can usually initiate foreclosure at a time specified in the mortgage documents, typically some period of time after a default condition occurs. Within the United States, Canada and many other countries, several types of foreclosure exist. In the U.S., two of them – namely, by judicial sale and by power of sale – are widely used, but other modes of foreclosure are also possible in a few states.

Foreclosure by judicial sale, more commonly known as *judicial foreclosure,* which is available in every state (and required in many), involves the sale of the mortgaged property under the supervision of a court, with the proceeds going first to satisfy the mortgage; then other lien holders; and, finally, the mortgagor/borrower if any proceeds are left. Under this system, the lender initiates foreclosure by filing a lawsuit against the borrower. As with all other legal actions, all parties must be notified of the foreclosure, but notification requirements vary significantly from state to state. A judicial decision is announced after the exchange of pleadings at a (usually short) hearing in a state or local court. In some rather rare instances, foreclosures are filed in federal courts.

Foreclosure by power of sale, also known as *non-judicial foreclosure,* is authorized by many states if a *power of sale* clause is included in the mortgage or if a deed of trust with such a clause was used, instead of an actual mortgage. In some states, like California, nearly all so-called mortgages are actually deeds of trust. This process involves the sale of the property by the mortgage holder without court supervision (as elaborated upon below). This process is generally much faster and cheaper than foreclosure by judicial sale. As in judicial sale, the mortgage holder and other lien holders are respectively first and second claimants to the proceeds from the sale.

Other types of foreclosure are considered minor because of their limited availability. Under *strict foreclosure,* which is available in a few states including Connecticut, New Hampshire and Vermont, suit is brought by the mortgagee and if successful, a court orders the defaulted mortgagor to pay the mortgage within a specified period of time. Should the mortgagor fail to do so, the mortgage holder gains the title to the property with no obligation to sell it. This type of foreclosure is generally available only when the value of the property is less than the debt ("under water"). Historically, strict foreclosure was the original method of foreclosure.

What is the Process?

The process of foreclosure can be rapid or lengthy and varies from state to state. Other options such as refinancing, a short sale, alternate financing, loan modification with the lender, or even bankruptcy may present homeowners with ways to avoid foreclosure. Websites which can connect individual borrowers and homeowners to lenders are increasingly offered as mechanisms to bypass traditional lenders while meeting payment obligations for mortgage providers. Although there are slight differences between the states, the foreclosure process generally follows a timeline beginning with initial missed payments, moving to a sale being scheduled and finally a redemption period (if available).

BANKRUPTCY... WHAT DO ALL THOSE CHAPTER'S MEAN?

CHAPTER 7: Liquidation Bankruptcy or "Fresh Start" Bankruptcy. Under this Bankruptcy Code you may protect exempt assets but most all other debt is removed. You may keep your home, mortgages on the property will remain. It is usually a 4 to 6 month process. It can delay Property Sale Dates but not indefinitely. Court filing fees and credit counseling required.

The Case is administered by a Bankruptcy Trustee with a required trustee supervised hearing with creditors that occurs roughly a month after filing. Debts that likely will not be removed are Student Loans, Divorce payments and child support. Chapter 7 can only be filed once every 8 years. Spouses can file separately. In order to qualify for Chapter 7 client must pass Bankruptcy Court's Means Test. Those who don't qualify based on income may qualify for Chapter 13 or 11.

CHAPTER 13: "Reorganization" bankruptcy. Commonly used to stop foreclosure, stop IRS collection (garnishments) or to consolidate debts into a single monthly affordable payment. Repayment plan for individuals with regular income and unsecured debt less than $336,900 and secured debt less than

$1,010,650. Court filing fees and credit counseling required. (credit counseling can be performed online for a small fee)

The Case is administered by a Bankruptcy Trustee with a required trustee supervised hearing with creditors that occurs roughly a month after filing. Typically a 5 year – 60 months payment plan is put in place until discharge. Non-Dischargeable debts can be put into a payment plan – Arrears from non-payment of mortgages for example. No limit of amount of times you can file Chapter 13, though most Courts discourage repetitive filings within a short period of time. You must meet monthly income requirements to qualify for Chapter 13. Sources of income can include: W2 or self-employment, social security income, pensions, among others.

CHAPTER 11: Individual, Sole Proprietorship or Corporate Reorganization Bankruptcy generally above $1.1 million in secured debt. There is no time limit on the repayment plan. It involves much more detailed legal, accounting, and trustee work therefore can be a more expensive options for clients.

Before filing Bankruptcy, you may want to consult with a financial advisor or an attorney to explore all your legal options.

SAMPLE HARDSHIP LETTER 1

January 1, 2012

To: Wells Fargo

Re: Loan Account Number:

To Whom it may Concern:

Due to the recent adjustment in the mortgage I currently have with your company, I am finding it very difficult to afford the new payment. I have a 5 year ARM which is now adjustable and is scheduled to adjust again in May, 2012.

Considering my current income, there will be no way I can afford the increased payments in May. Hopefully there is a way to renegotiate the terms of my current mortgage to avoid default and help stop foreclosure on my home.

Is it possible to have my current adjustable rate mortgage converted to a fixed rate? If this is not possible, can you postpone the next rate change to a future date to allow me to continue making affordable payments or refinance? Any other solutions you could provide would be greatly appreciated.

I have had no problem making my payments for over three years now and do not want that to change. My mortgage was originally written by another company and bought by Wells Fargo. I was assured that refinancing would be no problem but that turned out not to be true due to the downturn of the housing industry.

The main problem is that my property is now worth about 60% less than what I paid for it, which is preventing me from being able to refinance.

I believe this will address the situation I currently find myself in along with many other homeowners.

Thank you for your time and consideration.

Sincerely,

Your Signature
Co-Borrower's Signature

SAMPLE HARDSHIP LETTER 2

January 1, 2012

To: Bank of America

Re: Loan Account Number:

To Whom it may Concern:

The purpose of this letter is to explain the unfortunate set of circumstances that have led to my mortgage delinquency (or proposed delinquency, if not yet late). In December of 2011, I was laid off after my company went under. After exhausting all of my resources, I have but one avenue left, and that is to appeal to you for a mortgage loan modification. I believe this would be a tremendous relief in my situation in that it would allow me/us to affordably keep the home I/we/my family loves.

The main reason that caused me/us to be late (***insert reason here and don't be too lengthy or too vague. Please be sure to indicate the type of loan you have, if it is going to adjust, or has already adjusted, especially note if this is what created the hardship***). This has caused me to become further and further behind. I am not in the position to refinance due to the loss of values in the real estate market. (***Insert the approximate date of hardship and clarify if your situation is temporary or permanent***)

By obtaining a loan modification, I feel confident that I will be able to maintain my mortgage, and pay on the loan that has been afforded to me. I hope you will consider working with me/us on this matter.

Sincerely,

Your Signature
Co-Borrower's Signature

MORTGAGE GLOSSARY
OF TERMS

A-Credit: A consumer with the best credit rating, deserving of the lowest prices that lenders offer. Most lenders require a FICO score above 720. There is seldom any payoff for being above the A-credit threshold, but you pay a penalty for being below it.

Acceleration Clause: A contractual provision that gives the lender the right to demand repayment of the entire loan balance in the event that the borrower violates one or more clauses in the note.

Accrued Interest: Interest that is earned but not paid, adding to the amount owed.

Adjustable Rate Mortgage (ARM): A mortgage on which the interest rate, after an initial period, can be changed by the lender. While ARMs in many countries abroad allow rate changes at the lender's discretion, in the US most ARMs base rate changes on a pre-selected interest rate index over which the lender has no control.

Affordability: A consumer's capacity to afford a house. Affordability is usually expressed in terms of the maximum price the consumer could pay for a house, and be approved for the mortgage required to pay that amount.

Agreement of Sale: A contract signed by buyer and seller stating the terms and conditions under which a property will be sold.

Alt-A: A mortgage risk categorization that falls between prime and sub-prime, but is closer to prime. Also referred to as "A minus".

Alternative Documentation: Expedited and simpler documentation requirements designed to speed up the loan approval process. Instead of verifying employment with the applicant's employer and bank deposits with the applicant's bank, the lender will accept paycheck stubs, W-2s, and the borrower's original bank statements. Alternative documentation remains "full documentation", as opposed to the other documentation options.

Amortization: The repayment of principal from scheduled mortgage payments that exceed the interest due.

Amount financed: On the Truth in Lending form, the loan amount less "prepaid finance charges", which are lender fees paid at closing. For example, if the loan is for $100,000 and the borrower pays the lender $4,000 in fees, the amount financed is $96,000.

Annual percentage rate (APR): See APR.

Application: A request for a loan that includes the information about the potential borrower, the property and the requested loan that the solicited lender needs to make a decision. In a narrower sense, the application refers to a standardized application form called the "1003" which the borrower is obliged to fill out.

Application fee: A fee that some lenders charge to accept an application. It may or may not cover other costs such as a property appraisal or credit report, and it may or may not be refundable if the lender declines the loan.

Appraisal: A written estimate of a property's current market value prepared by an appraiser.

Appraiser: A professional with knowledge of real estate markets and skilled in the practice of appraisal. When a property is appraised in connection with a loan, the appraiser is selected by the lender, but the appraisal fee is usually paid by the borrower.

Appraisal fee: A fee charged by an appraiser for the appraisal of a particular property.

APR: The Annual Percentage Rate, which must be reported by lenders under Truth in Lending regulations. It is a measure of credit cost to the borrower that takes account of the interest rate, points, and flat dollar charges by the lender. The charges covered by the APR also include mortgage insurance premiums, but not other payments to third parties, such as payments to title insurers or appraisers. The APR is adjusted for the time value of money, so that dollars paid by the borrower up-front carry a heavier weight than dollars paid in the future.

ARM: An adjustable rate mortgage.

Assumption: A method of selling real estate where the buyer of the property agrees to become responsible for the repayment of an existing loan on the property. Unless the lender also agrees, however, the seller remains liable for the mortgage.

Assumable mortgage: A mortgage contract that allows, or does not prohibit, a creditworthy buyer from assuming the mortgage contract of the seller. Assuming a loan will save the buyer money if the rate on the existing loan is below the current market rate, and closing costs are avoided as well.

Automated underwriting: A computer-driven process for informing the loan applicant very quickly, sometimes within a few minutes, whether the applicant will be approved, or whether the application will be forwarded to an underwriter. The quick decision is based on information provided by the applicant, who is subject to later verification, and other information retrieved electronically including information about the borrower's credit history and the subject property.

Bad-faith estimate: The practice of low-balling figures for settlement costs on the Good Faith Estimate to make them appear more attractive to mortgage shoppers.

Bail-Out: Government support to a firm in trouble, which is usually limited to protecting creditors and employees.

Balance: The amount of the original loan remaining to be paid. It is equal to the loan amount less the sum of all prior payments of principal.

Balloon mortgage: A mortgage which is payable in full after a period that is shorter than the term. In most cases, the balance is refinanced with the current or another lender. On a 7-year balloon loan, for example, the payment is usually calculated over a 30-year period, and the balance at the end of the 7th year must be repaid or refinanced at that time. Balloon mortgages are similar to ARMs in that the borrower trades off a lower rate in the early years against the risk of a higher rate later. They are riskier than ARMs because there is no limit on the extent of a rate increase at the end of the balloon period.

Balloon: The loan balance remaining at the time the loan contract calls for full repayment.

Bridge loan: A short-term loan, usually from a bank, that "bridges" the period between the closing date of a home purchase and the closing date of a home sale. Unsecured bridge loans are available if the borrower has a firm contract to sell the existing house. Secured bridge loans are available without such a contract.

Buy-down: A permanent buy-down is the payment of points in exchange for a lower interest rate.

Cash-Out refi: Refinancing for an amount in excess of the balance on the old loan plus settlement costs. The borrower takes "cash-out" of the transaction. This way of raising cash is usually an alternative to taking out a home equity loan.

Cash-in refi: As part of a refinance transaction, paying down the loan balance in order to reduce the loan-to-value ratio and qualify for a lower interest rate and/or reduced mortgage insurance premium.

Closing: On a home purchase, the process of transferring ownership from the seller to the buyer, the disbursement of funds from the buyer and the lender to the seller, and the execution of all the documents associated with the sale and the loan. On a refinance, there is no transfer of ownership, but the closing includes repayment of the old lender.

Closing costs: Same as Settlement costs.

Closing date: The date on which the closing occurs.

Co-Borrowers: One or more persons who have signed the note, and are equally responsible for repaying the loan. Unmarried co-borrowers who live together are advised to agree beforehand on what happens if they split.

Construction financing: The method of financing used when a borrower contracts to have a house built as opposed to purchasing a completed house

Conventional mortgage: A home mortgage that is neither FHA-insured nor VA-guaranteed.

Conversion option: The option to convert an ARM to an FRM at some point during its life. These loans are likely to carry a higher rate or points than ARMs that do not have the option.

Co-signing a note: Assuming responsibility for someone else's loan in the event that that party defaults. A risk not to be taken lightly.

Credit report: A report from a credit bureau containing detailed information bearing on credit-worthiness, including the individual's credit history.

Credit score: A single numerical score, based on an individual's credit history, which measures that individual's credit worthiness. Credit scores are as good as the algorithm used to derive them. The most widely used credit score is called FICO for Fair Isaac Co. which developed it.

Debt consolidation: Rolling short-term debt into a home mortgage loan, either at the time of home purchase or later.

Debt elimination: Scams designed to relieve you of your money by promising to eliminate your mortgage debt.

Deed in lieu of foreclosure: Deeding the property over to the lender as an alternative to having the lender foreclose on the property.

Default: Failure of the borrower to honor the terms of the loan agreement. Lenders (and the law) usually view borrowers delinquent 90 days or more as in default.

Delinquency: A mortgage payment that is more than 30 days late.

Demand clause: A clause in the note that allows the lender to demand repayment at any time for any reason.

Discount mortgage broker: A mortgage broker who claims to be compensated entirely by the lender rather than by the borrower.

Discretionary ARM: An adjustable rate mortgage on which the lender has the right to change the interest rate at any time subject only to advance notice.

Documentation requirements: The set of lender requirements that specify how information about a loan applicant's income and assets must be provided, and how it will be used by the lender.

Down payment: The difference between the value of the property and the loan amount, expressed in dollars, or as a percentage of the price. For example, if the house sells for $100,000 and the loan is for $80,000, the down payment is $20,000 or 20%.

Due-on-sale clause: A provision of a loan contract that stipulates that if the property is sold the loan balance must be repaid. This bars the seller from transferring responsibility for an existing loan to the buyer when the interest rate on the old loan is below the current market. A mortgage containing a due-on-sale clause is not an assumable mortgage.

Effective rate: A term used in two ways. In one context it refers to a measure of interest cost to the borrower that is identical to the APR except that it is calculated over the time horizon specified by the borrower. The APR is calculated on the assumption that the loan runs to term, which most loans do not.

Equity: In connection with a home, the difference between the value of the home and the balance of outstanding mortgage loans on the home.

Escrow: An agreement that money or other objects of value be placed with a third party for safe keeping, pending the performance of some promised act by one of the parties to the agreement.

Fees: The sum of all upfront cash payments required by the lender as part of the charge for the loan. Origination fees and points are expressed as a percent of the loan. Junk fees are expressed in dollars.

FHA mortgage: A mortgage on which the lender is insured against loss by the Federal Housing Administration, with the borrower paying the mortgage insurance premium. The major advantage of an FHA mortgage is that the required down payment.

FICO Score: See Credit Score. Your Credit Score ranking.

First mortgage: A mortgage that has a first-priority claim against the property in the event the borrower defaults on the loan. For example, a borrower defaults on a loan secured by a property worth $100,000 net of sale costs. The property has a first mortgage with a balance of $90,000 and a second mortgage with a balance of $15,000. The first mortgage lender can collect $90,000 plus any unpaid interest and foreclosure costs. The second mortgage lender can collect only what is left of the $100,000.

Fixed rate mortgage (FRM): A mortgage on which the interest rate and monthly mortgage payment remain unchanged throughout the term of the mortgage.

Float: Allowing the rate and points to vary with changes in market conditions. The borrower may elect to lock the rate and points at any time but must do so a few days before the closing. Allowing the rate to float exposes the borrower to market risk, and also to the risk of being taken advantage of by the loan provider.

Float-down: A rate lock, plus an option to reduce the rate if market interest rates decline during the lock period. Also called a cap. A float-down costs the borrower more than a lock because it is more costly to the lender. Float-downs vary widely in terms of how often the borrower can exercise (usually only once), and exactly when the borrower can exercise.

Foreclosure: The legal process by which a lender acquires possession of the property securing a mortgage loan when the borrower defaults.

Forbearance agreement: An agreement by the lender not to exercise the legal right to foreclose in exchange for an agreement by the borrower to a payment plan that will cure the borrower's delinquency.

Front-end fee: Mortgage broker income paid by the borrower, as distinguished from the fee paid by the lender, which is "back-end".

Fully amortizing payment: The monthly mortgage payment which, if maintained unchanged through the remaining life of the loan at the then-existing interest rate, will pay off the loan over the remaining life.

Gift of equity: A sale price below market value, where the difference is a gift from the sellers to the buyers. Such gifts are usually between family members. Lenders will usually allow the gift to count as down payment.

Good faith estimate: The form that lists the settlement charges the borrower must pay at closing, which the lender is obliged to provide the borrower within three business days of receiving the loan application.

Grace period: The period after the payment due date during which the borrower can pay without being hit for late fees. Grace periods apply only to mortgages on which interest is calculated monthly.

Hazard insurance: Insurance purchased by the borrower, and required by the lender, to protect the property against loss from fire and other hazards. Also known as "homeowner insurance", it is the second "I" in PITI.

HECM: Stands for Home Equity Conversion Mortgage, a reverse mortgage program authorized by Congress in 1988. On a HECM, FHA insures the lender against loss in the event the loan balance at termination exceeds the value of the property, and insures the borrower that any payments due from the lender will be made, even if the lender fails.

Homebuyer protection plan: A plan purporting to protect FHA homebuyers against property defects.

Homeowner's equity: See Equity.

Homeowners insurance: Insurance purchased by the borrower, and required by the lender, to protect the property against loss from fire and other hazards. It is the second "I" in PITI.

Home equity line of credit (HELOC): A mortgage set up as a line of credit against which a borrower can draw up to a maximum amount, as opposed to a loan for a fixed dollar amount. For example, using a standard mortgage you might borrow $150,000, which would be paid out in its entirety at closing. Using a HELOC instead, you receive the lender's promise to advance you up to $150,000, in an amount and at a time of your choosing. You can draw on the line by writing a check, using a special credit card, or in other ways.

Home Equity Conversion Mortgage (HECM): A reverse mortgage program administered by FHA.

Housing bubble: A marked increase in house prices fueled partly by expectations that prices will continue to rise.

HUD1 form: The form a borrower receives at closing that details all the payments and receipts among the parties in a real estate transaction, including borrower, lender, home seller, mortgage broker and various other service providers.

Hybrid ARM: An ARM on which the initial rate holds for some period, during which it is "fixed-rate", after which it becomes adjustable rate. Generally, the term is applied to ARMs with initial rate periods of 3 years or longer.

Initial interest rate: The interest rate that is fixed for some specified number of months at the beginning of the life of a an ARM.

Initial rate period: The number of months for which the initial rate holds, ranging from 1 month to 10 years.

Interest accrual period: The period over which the interest due the lender is calculated.

Interest cost: A time-adjusted measure of cost to a mortgage borrower. It is calculated in the same way as the APR except that the APR assumes that the loan runs to term, and is always measured before taxes.

Interest due: The amount of interest, expressed in dollars, computed by multiplying the loan balance at the end of the preceding period times the annual interest rate divided by the interest accrual period.

Interest-only mortgage: A mortgage on which for some period the monthly mortgage payment consists of interest only. During that period, the loan balance remains unchanged.

Interest payment: The dollar amount of interest paid each month. It is the same as interest due so long as the scheduled mortgage payment is equal to or greater than the interest due. Otherwise, the interest payment is equal to the scheduled payment.

Interest rate: The rate charged the borrower each period for the loan of money, by custom quoted on an annual basis. A rate of

6%, for example, means a rate of 1/2% per month. A mortgage interest rate is a rate on a loan secured by a specific property.

Investor: In real estate, a borrower who owns or purchases a property as an investment rather than as a residence.

Junk fees: A derogatory term for lender fees expressed in dollars rather than as a percent of the loan amount.

Late fees: Fees that lenders are entitled to collect from borrowers who don't pay within the grace period.

Lease-to-own purchase: A transaction in which a hopeful home buyer leases a home with an option to buy it within a specified period.

Lender: See Mortgage Lender.

Lien: The lender's right to claim the borrower's property in the event the borrower defaults. If there is more than one lien, the claim of the lender holding the first lien will be satisfied before the claim of the lender holding the second lien, which in turn will be satisfied before the claim of a lender holding a third lien, etc.

Loan amount: The amount the borrower promises to repay, as set forth in the mortgage contract. It differs from the amount of cash disbursed by the lender by the amount of points and other upfront costs included in the loan.

Loan modification: See Mortgage Modification.

Loan officer: Employees of lenders or mortgage brokers who find borrowers, sell and counsel them, and take applications.

Loan provider: A lender or mortgage broker.

Loan-to-value ratio: The loan amount divided by the lesser of the selling price or the appraised value. Also referred to as LTV. The LTV and down payment are different ways of expressing the same set of facts.

Mandatory disclosure: The array of laws and regulations dictating the information that must be disclosed to mortgage borrowers, and the method and timing of disclosure.

Manufactured housing: A house built entirely in a factory, transported to a site and installed there. They are usually built without knowing where they will be sited, and are subject to a Federal building code administered by HUD.

Margin: The amount added to the interest rate index, ranging generally from 2 to 3 percentage points, to obtain the fully indexed interest rate on an ARM.

Market niche: A particular combination of loan, borrower and property characteristics that lenders use in setting prices and underwriting requirements. These characteristics are believed to affect the default risk or cost of the loan. As examples, borrowers who don't intend to occupy the house they purchase pay more than those who do, and borrowers who refinance only the balance on their existing loan pay less than those who take "cash out".

Maturity: The period until the last payment is due. This is usually but not always the term, which is the period used to calculate the mortgage payment.

Maximum loan amount: The largest loan size permitted on a particular loan program.

Maximum loan to value ratio: The maximum allowable loan-to-value ratio on the selected loan program.

Mortgage: A written document evidencing the lien on a property taken by a lender as security for the repayment of a loan. The term "mortgage" or "mortgage loan" is used loosely to refer both to the lien and the loan. In most cases, they are defined in two separate documents: a mortgage and a note.

Mortgage bank: Same as mortgage company.

Mortgage broker: An independent contractor who offers the loan products of multiple lenders, termed wholesalers. A mortgage broker counsels on the loans available from different wholesalers, takes the application, and usually processes the loan. When the file is complete, but sometimes sooner, the lender underwrites the loan. In contrast to a correspondent, a mortgage broker does not fund a loan.

Mortgage company: A mortgage lender who sells all loans in the secondary market. As distinguished from a portfolio lender, who retains loans in its portfolio. Mortgage companies may or may not service the loans they originate.

Mortgage insurance: Insurance against loss provided to a mortgage lender in the event of borrower default where the borrower pays the premiums.

Mortgage insurance premium: The up-front and/or periodic charges that the borrower pays for mortgage insurance. There are different mortgage insurance plans with differing combinations of up-front, monthly and annual premiums. The most widely used premium plan is a monthly charge with no upfront premium.

Mortgage lender: The party who disburses funds to the borrower at the closing table. The lender receives the note evidencing the borrower's indebtedness and obligation to repay, and the mortgage which is the lien on the subject property.

Mortgage modification: A change in the terms of a loan, usually the interest rate and/or term, in response to the borrower's inability to make the payments under the existing contract.

Mortgage payment: The monthly payment of interest and principal made by the borrower.

Negative Homeowners Equity: The condition of owing more on the house than the house is worth.

No-cost mortgage: A mortgage on which all settlement costs except per diem interest, escrows, homeowners insurance and transfer taxes are paid by the lender and/or the home seller.

No asset loan: A documentation requirement where the applicant's assets are not disclosed. See

No Fee Mortgage Plus: A Bank of America program for home purchasers that eliminates all lender fees except points, and all third party fees.

No income loan: A documentation requirement where the applicant's income is not disclosed.

Option ARM: An adjustable rate mortgage with flexible payment options, monthly interest rate adjustments, and very low minimum payments in the early years. They carry a risk of very large payments in later years.

Origination fee: An upfront fee charged by some lenders, usually expressed as a percent of the loan amount. It should be added to points in determining the total fees charged by the lender that are expressed as a percent of the loan amount. Unlike points, however, an origination fee does not vary with the interest rate.

Piggyback mortgage: A combination of a first mortgage for 80% of property value, and a second for 5%, 10%, 15%, or 20% of value. These combinations are designated as 80/5/15, 80/10/10, 80/15/5, and 80/20/0, respectively. Piggybacks are a substitute for mortgage insurance for borrowers who cannot put 20% down.

PITI: Shorthand for principal, interest, taxes and insurance, which are the components of the monthly housing expense.

PMI: Private mortgage insurance, as distinguished from insurance provided by government under FHA.

Points: An upfront cash payment required by the lender as part of the charge for the loan.

Pre-approval: A commitment by a lender to make a mortgage loan to a specified borrower, prior to the identification of a specific property. It is designed to make it easier to shop for a house. Unlike a pre-qualification, the lender checks the applicant's credit.

Prepayment penalty: A charge imposed by the lender if the borrower pays off the loan early. The charge is usually expressed as a percent of the loan balance at the time of prepayment, or a specified number of months interest.

Primary residence: The house in which the borrower will live most of the time, as distinct from a second home or an investor property that will be rented.

Principal: The portion of the monthly payment that is used to reduce the loan balance.

Processing: Compiling and maintaining the file of information about a mortgage transaction, including the credit report, appraisal, verification of employment and assets, and so on. The processing file is handed off to underwriting for the loan decision.

Qualification: The process of determining whether a prospective borrower has the ability, meaning sufficient assets and income, to repay a loan. Qualification is sometimes referred to as "pre-qualification" because it is subject to verification of the information provided by the applicant.

Rate: See Interest Rate.

Rate sheets: Tables of interest rates and points that lenders distribute daily to their loan officer employees or mortgage brokers.

Refinance: Paying off an old loan while simultaneously taking a new one. This may be done to reduce borrowing costs under conditions where the borrower can obtain a new loan at an interest rate below the rate on the existing loan. It may be done to raise cash, as an alternative to a home equity loan. Or it may be done to reduce the monthly payment.

RESPA: The Real Estate Settlement Procedures Act, a Federal consumer protection statute first enacted in 1974. RESPA was designed to protect home purchasers and owners shopping for settlement services by mandating certain disclosures, and prohibiting referral fees and kickbacks.

Reverse mortgage: A loan to parties over 62 years of age. In which loan is not repaid until the owner dies, sells the house, or moves out permanently.

Right of rescission: The right of refinancing borrowers, under the Truth in Lending Act, to cancel the deal at no cost to themselves within 3 days of closing.

Second mortgage: A loan with a second-priority claim against a property in the event that the borrower defaults. The lender who holds the second mortgage gets paid only after the lender holding the first mortgage is paid.

Seller contribution: A contribution to a borrower's down payment or settlement costs made by a home seller, as an alternative to a price reduction.

Seller financing: Provision of a mortgage by the seller of a house, often a second mortgage, as a condition of the sale.

Short sale: An agreement between a mortgagor (borrower) in distress and the lender that allows the borrower to sell the house for less than what he/she owes and remit the proceeds to the lender. It is an alternative to foreclosure, or a deed in lieu of foreclosure.

Silent second: A second mortgage used to deceive the first mortgage lender, or to provide preferential (subsidized) terms to qualified home buyers.

Simple interest mortgage: A mortgage on which interest is calculated daily based on the balance at the time of the last payment. The daily interest charge within the month is constant -- interest is not charged on the interest charges of prior days.

Stated income: A documentation requirement where the lender verifies the source of the income but not the amount.

Streamlined refinancing: Refinancing that omits some of the standard risk control measures, and is therefore quicker and less costly.

Sub-prime borrower: A borrower with poor credit, who can borrow only from sub-prime lenders who specialize in dealing with borrowers who have poor credit. Such borrowers pay more than prime borrowers, and are sometimes taken advantage of. Not all borrowers who deal with sub-prime lenders, however, are sub-prime borrowers. Some could obtain loans from mainstream lenders if they properly shop the market.

Sub-prime lender: A lender who specializes in lending to sub-prime borrowers.

Sub-prime market: The network of sub-prime lenders, mortgage brokers, warehouse lenders and investment bankers who make possible the delivery of loans to sub-prime borrowers.

Temporary buy down: A reduction in the mortgage payment in the early years of the loan in exchange for an upfront cash payment provided by the home buyer, the seller, or both.

Term: The period used to calculate the monthly mortgage payment. The term is usually but not always the same as the maturity.

Title insurance: Insurance against loss arising from problems connected to the title to property.

Truth in Lending (TIL): The Federal law that specifies the information that must be provided to borrowers on different types of loans. Also, the form used to disclose this information.

Underwriting: The process of examining all the data about a borrower's property and transaction to determine whether the mortgage applied for by the borrower should be issued. The person who does this is called an underwriter.

Underwriting requirements: The standards imposed by lenders in determining whether a borrower qualifies for a loan. These standards are more comprehensive than qualification requirements in that they include an evaluation of the borrower's creditworthiness.

VA mortgage: A mortgage with no down payment requirement, available only to ex-servicemen and women as well as those on active duty, on which the lender is insured against loss by the Veterans Administration.

Wrap-around mortgage: A mortgage on a property that already has a mortgage, where the new lender assumes the payment obligation on the old mortgage. Wrap-around mortgages arise when the current market rate is above the rate on the existing mortgage, and home sellers are frequently the lender.

LOAN MODIFICATION PROGRAMS

HAMP – President Obama's Making Home Affordable. Qualifications are reducing your payment if your payment exceeds 31% of your gross income. Here is an example.

Ex: 5,000.00 (gross income) x 31% = $1,550.00 If your mortgage payment is higher than $1,550.00 you are half way to qualification status.

CHAMP – Chase Banks in-house program. If one does not qualify for the HAMP program Chased will try and qualify you for the CHAMP. Guidelines are similar to the HAMP, however the hardship is taken in to consideration and approval process is more flexible.

In-house Programs – Each bank has their own set of rules. It is possible that your bank can offer you an in-house program. If you have been denied for a HAMP ask your bank to consider you for their in-house program where guidelines can be more flexible.

HARP – Refinance Program – offered if your home is up-side-down. Rates are low take advantage of this program while you can! For loans held by Fannie Mae only. See a mortgage professional to see if you qualify.

HARP 2.0 – Refinance Program for homes underwater including Investment properties.

FHA – Streamline available to all homes underwater. Fast and easy process no documentation required and no appraisal required.

Repayment Program – your lender will take the total amount in arrears and break it down into 5 payments. The payments will bring you to a "current" status. Generally, the payments will be close to your initial payment if not higher.

Forbearance – a Max 6 month program. Your mortgage will be cut in half for up to 6 months. At the end of six months the remaining balance of arrearage will be due immediately similar to a balloon note.

Partial Claim – For FHA loans only. The arrearage will be placed onto the back of loan. Mortgagee will advance funds on behalf of a mortgagor to reinstate delinquent loan.

Deed in Lieu – relief of title to the lender, voluntary repossession. Whereas the mortgagor gives back the keys to the lender without recourse. Shows better on credit as opposed to a foreclosure.

MORTGAGE LOANS AVAILABLE

- Conventional – purchase /refinance (and homes under water)
- FHA – .5% down and 3.5% down
- VA – "0" down payment 100% financing
- USDA "0" 100% no money down seller pays all closing
- REVERSE Mortgage
- Jumbo loans up to 3 million
- Super Jumbo – call for details
- Hard money – great for real estate investors

- Bridge loans for Short Sales

   If you cannot afford your mortgage payment while going through the short sale process, and would like to preserve your good credit rating, obtain a bridge loan. This loan will pay the mortgage while you sale your home and relieve you from denting your credit history.

- Did you know???

   Did you know you could purchase a home immediately after the short sale of your home? Yes…it's true. There is a catch in that you MUST purchase with a FHA loan, but the option is available in the event you chose to purchase instead of rent. 1 day out of the short sale and you are ready to purchase your next home.

MEET THE AUTHOR

Kelly Rivas a native of California prides herself on her superior customer service coupled with her expertise in the Real Estate and Mortgage Industry. With over 20 years of experience as a Realtor, Broker, Real estate Investor, and Mortgage Branch Manager with such skills that needs no embellishment, Kelly has proven to be a powerful force in the industry.

Kelly finds her greatest satisfaction in meeting the needs of her clients in a friendly and professional manner. At the end of the day Kelly describes her role as a Broker as a people business, not a transaction. She strives to complete every transaction for her clients while obtaining the strictest compliance in accordance with RESPA guidelines.

Kelly's goal is not only to satisfy her customers, but to also educate them in the process!

Helpful Links

http://www.makinghomeaffordable.gov

For Harp program - to find if you are eligible for a HARP go to:
http://www.fanniemae.com/loanlookup
http://www.freddiemac.com/
http://www.fha.com/hope_for_homeowners.cfm
http://www.hud.gov
http://www.hopenow.com